Isle of Wight
Gem of the Solent

written by June Elford
with photographs by Steve Gascoigne

Bird's-eye view of the Needles

Isle of Wight
Gem of the Solent

written by June Elford
with photographs by Steve Gascoigne

WILD
ISLES
Series

COACH HOUSE PUBLICATIONS
ISLE OF WIGHT
ENGLAND

Front Cover Photograph, Compton Bay.

ISBN: 1-899-392-335
First Printing November 2004

COACH HOUSE PUBLICATIONS LIMITED

ISLE OF WIGHT, ENGLAND

The Coach House, School Green Road, Freshwater, Isle of Wight, PO40 9BB
Tel: +44 (0) 1983 755655

Further copies of this book can be obtained from the publishers by contacting us at the address above
or via our online ordering service at www.coachhouseonline.co.uk

Printed in the UK by LPC Printing Ltd
Book Design by David Bowles

Table OF Contents

From the cliff top, Watcombe Bay looks remote but there's a tunnel to the caves hidden below and the shore.

Introduction & Acknowledgements

A guide published in 1889 said of the Isle of Wight, "Few places are more celebrated and praised for the beauty of both inland and coast scenery."

So what's so special about this diamond-shaped island off the south coast of England? Is it the way the surrounding sea sets it physically apart from the mainland or the distinct feeling visitors experience of embarking on a holiday abroad without the need for a passport or phrasebook? Or is it a sense of just-past, the British seaside of the Fifties with candy floss, sandcastles and deckchairs, donkey rides and crazy golf.

Perhaps we should look at a few facts? The Isle of Wight is the largest political constituency in the country but the smallest county in England. It has more miles of public footpath than public road, 30 miles of heritage coastline with half of the Island's 94,000 acres designated as an Area of Outstanding Natural Beauty.

The Island is packed with a variety of cliffs and forests, green valleys and broad-backed downs, sandy bays and Victorian seaside resorts. There are warnings of 'Squirrels!' and 'Island roads are different' on road signs, and honesty boxes at the garden gates for the vegetables and flowers on sale.

Five thousand years ago the Island was joined to the British mainland. Then the sea broke through and created a narrow stretch of water called the Solent. Now this gem of an island sits comfortably in the English Channel with the sea chipping away at its shores, a coastal protection nightmare for the local community and a palaeontologist's paradise of fossils.

A character in Jane Austin's *'Mansfield Park'*, says "she thinks of nothing but the Isle of Wight, and she calls it *the Island,* as if there were no other island in the world". Islanders are the same and, although its small size means distances are short, people have been known to gasp and turn pale at the thought of travelling the twenty odd miles from east to west Wight - as if they'd been asked to go to Tierra del Fuego.

The Victorians in their horse-drawn carriages toured the Island in a clockwise direction but this book isn't meant to be a nob's view of history so we're going on an armchair journey anticlockwise starting with Ryde.

Special thanks go to Tony Hall of Coach House Publications for his patience and good humour, to my editor, Diana Kimpton, for her help and encouragement and to Steve Gascoigne, our photographer. Also thanks to the many people who answered questions and gave me their time, especially Roy Brinton, Diana Harding, Martin Woodward, Lauri Say, John Hannan, Brian Hinton, Dr. Colin Pope and the staff at the Isle of Wight Coastal Visitors Centre.

June Elford

CHAPTER ONE

By Bus to Cowes

Seen from the ferry, Ryde pier is a long black finger pointing to the mainland. Anyone visiting Ryde before the pier was built in 1814, faced the prospect of being transferred from a boat called a wherry into a horse and cart, or being piggy-backed over the mud to the shore. Now a railway runs the length of the pier, the fourth longest in the country and onwards to Lake, Sandown and Shanklin.

The addition of a tramway in the 1860s made Ryde pier unusual as its three independent piers were joined at both the sea end and land end. A first class ticket on the tramway cost 2p, second class 1p and its demise was sadly mourned when it was dismantled in 1969 and an ex-London underground train waits at the pierhead to rattle the ferry passengers half a mile down the pier to the Esplanade.

La Riche or La Rye as the Normans knew Ryde, grew out of two hamlets, one on the hill and the other by the sea. Later the two were joined by Union Street and with the growth of the railways, Ryde soon rivalled Brighton and Bath as a fashionable holiday resort. Gibbs and Gurnell, a chemist shop at the top of Union Street dispensed medicines to Queen Victoria who was soon to build her summer home on the Island, the much loved Osborne House.

On the seafront, Ryde's Eastern Esplanade juggles between new and old. The hovercraft arrives and departs in a flurry of spray and the jingling halyards on the yachts in the marina mingle with the strains of "Oh, My darling Clementine" from a monster bouncy castle. Ryde Pavilion suits the

On the beach at Binstead before the path to Quarr
turns inland through the woods.

Stretching half a mile out to sea, Ryde Pier is the fourth longest in the country. Before it was built as a landing place for boats in 1814, visitors to the Island were transported to the shore by horse and cart.

Ripples in the sand on Ryde beach. The sea waits for the turn of the tide, ready to creep back and sweep away the sandcastles and the footprints in the sand.

The ornate iron railings on Ryde Pier are Edwardian, a time when it was fashionable to take a stroll along one of the first promenade piers to be built in Britain.

image of earlier days. Built by Walter Macfarlane in 1926 in kit form on a metal framework, a sort of early Meccano set, the pavilion is identical to one in Rothsay on the Isle of Bute, both having four corner towers with stained glass windows and delicate lacey ironwork on the roof.

Further along the Esplanade the swans on the boating-lake glide distainfully round a fleet of plastic swan boats with heads like first-century Phoenician merchant ships. In summer the flowerbeds blaze with mauve and crimson petunias and the muddy shore, problematic for those early travellers, has been refurbished with six miles of sparkling golden sand. At low tide the sea turns and meanders up the beach, forming creeks and pools before maliciously gathering speed and cutting off sandbanks and anyone unfortunate enough to be on them. For those who ignore the warning notices along the Esplanade, there's an Inshore Lifeboat Station and rescue boat, past the boating lake, at Appley Park manned by volunteers.

The Park used to belong to Sir William Hutt, MP and Paymaster General, who bought Appley Tower House in the mid-1870s and spent thousands of pounds improving the estate. Only Rapunzel is missing from the fairytale castellated tower he built near the shore where *'Vouloir est Pouvoir'*, is engraved on a shield above the door. I feel, 'To wish is all', sums up the character of the man who gave the land below the sea wall for the people of Ryde to enjoy, where Victorian ladies could enjoy picnics at the folly or venture modestly into the sea from the safety of a bathing machine.

Out to sea and northeast of the boomerang curve of the bay on No Man's Land shoal is a squat granite tower, one of three forts called 'Palmerston's Follies' built to defend Portsmouth against foreign warships. Though the antics of Napoleon 111 had caused temporary alarms in London, the Chancellor of the Exchequer, William Gladstone, didn't believe France would invade and threatened to resign over the cost of building the forts. History records Lord Palmerston's remark to Queen Victoria that if there was a choice, it would be preferable to lose Mr. Gladstone than to lose Portsmouth: it doesn't record Mr. Gladstone's reaction.

Work on No Man's Land fort began in 1865. Circular with armour plated walls, it had an artesian well for water, a basement and two other floors. Later the fort was used as a Naval Signal station and during the Second World War had a boom defence rigged between it and Horse Sand fort. Ironically, except during air raids in the last war, none of the forts ever had to fire a shot in anger.

In 1963 they were put up for sale and today No Man's Land fort must be one of the most unusual venues in England licensed for weddings. Couples can enjoy 'a stress-free occasion' in the Lighthouse honeymoon suite and the rooms where the soldiers slept in hammocks have been converted into a night-club and a disco; other creature comforts are the swimming pool, a roof garden and an Observatory with 360 degree views.

Back to the end of the pier and the bus terminus. The Island's bus company, Southern Vectis, had its image immortalized by Lauri Say in 1968 when he released his EP 'The Isle of Wight for Me', a collection of slightly satirical songs including the 'Southern Vectis Bus Song' with the refrain,

"Listen to the rumble, the racket and the din,
And listen to the jingle of the money rolling in.
Well, it's a public company and it's owned by all of us,
So make yourself a profit ride on a Southern Vectis bus."

The Company is now privately owned and according to a national newspaper article the Island has the best bus service in the country. Vectis, meaning "That which has arisen out of the sea" was the name the Roman emperor Vespasian gave the Isle of Wight in A.D. 43 and it was Christopher and Frank Dodson, the company's orignal partners, who thought up the nifty name for their growing fleet of buses. When some of the single-deck buses were requisitioned for military purposes during the early part of World War 11, the Company operated seven vehicles with gas-producing trailers to conserve fuel.

No Man's Land Fort is one of three forts built in 1865 by Lord Palmerston to defend Portsmouth's naval base against the French. Today the fort is one of the most unusual venues in England licensed for weddings.

Travelling on the upper deck of a bus from Ryde to East Cowes. I can look into people's gardens and see things I miss from a car as well as All Saints church at the top of the town which nobody could miss as its spire can be seen for miles. The church was designed by Sir George Gilbert Scott, architect and grandfather of Sir Giles Gilbert Scott, another genius who won a competition at the age of twenty-one to design the Anglican cathedral in Liverpool.

Unlike the rural west of the Island, the north-east is heavily populated and many of Ryde's residents commute to the mainland to work. Large Georgian and Victorian houses are surrounded by a suburban development that stretches to Binstead where I nip off the bus and into the churchyard of Holy Cross church to look at the sheela-na-gig, a grotesque fertility figure, known locally as "The Idol", set in an arch in the churchyard wall and close by the grave of Thomas Sivell, a ferryman, who according to the inscription on his headstone, was "cruelly shot on board his sloop by some officers of the custom" in 1785 when he was mistaken for a smuggler.

Back on the bus and coasting down Quarr Hill, I catch a glimpse of the sea and the ruined Cistercian abbey which Benedictine monks replaced in 1908 with a red brick abbey complex. Visitors are welcome to Quarr to take tea in the garden, visit the shop and browse over the pottery made by the monks and if you are near the Abbey at vespers, take the opportunity to hear them singing Gregorian chant in the half-lit vaulted nave of the abbey; I guarantee you'll never forget the experience.

Crossing the causeway at Wootton Creek I remembered my visit to Roland Rieul at his old hunting lodge in Firestone Copse. No one could have looked less like a spy than this gentle man in his quiet home but during the last war, he risked crossing the border between Switzerland and France 27 times to bring back important information for British Intelligence. Post-war, he was prouder of his snooker trophies than his Croix de Guerre medal and the commendation he received from Field Marshal Montgomery.

Built by Sir William Hutt as a folly, Appley Tower was a favourite picnic place for Victorian ladies. The bas-relief behind the tower commemorates *HMS Sirius*, a naval consort for the First Fleet which sailed to Australia on 13 May, 1787, and was wrecked on Norfolk Island.

At this point I'm going to indulge in a bit of misty romanticism and mention the legend I like about King's Quay near Wootton Creek. It claims that King John, feeling extremely disgruntled after his *contratemps* with the barons, came to King's Quay for rest and recuperation where he met and wooed an unknown lady. It's true that King John came to the Island and stayed at Yarmouth in 1206 and in 1214, but there's no proof that he stayed here or how the quay came by its name.

But there's no stopping there today either. Instead I'm en route for Osborne House, one of the jewels in English Heritage's crown. Built as a holiday home for Queen Victoria and Prince Albert's family to 'get away from it all', the house is not beautiful but the setting, which reminded Albert of the Bay of Naples, is magnificent. Albert may not have been good at designing houses but he had talent when it came to landscaping. He constructed Italianate terraces in two tiers at the rear of Osborne House, planted trees and made a sweeping valley to the sea. Victoria called her summer home 'a little paradise' and each spring she would send Disraeli huge baskets of primroses, his favourite flower, from the estate.

A short hop from Osborne is St. Mildred's church at Whippingham. It was designed by Nash but Prince Albert had a hand in it as he couldn't resist dabbling in architecture and there's a elaborate monument to him inside. There's a more modest one in the churchyard to Uffa Fox, yachtsman and naval architect, whose gravestone is illustrated with an airborne lifeboat floating down on three parachutes and the symbol of the Flying Fifteen dinghy, both designed by Uffa.

At one time Uffa lived for some time on the River Medina, the same river where his ancestor, William Robertson, had been a ferryman on the old East Cowes crossing. Uffa bought a 1896 chain ferry, one of a series that linked the two halves of Cowes for years, which he converted into living accommodation, a drawing office and workshop and to avoid paying rates Uffa often changed the boat's mooring without warning his wife that her home had been moved.

Built in 1937, the *Ryde* paddle steamer went into service on the Portsmouth to Ryde route. She helped with the rescue operation at Dunkirk in 1940 and was renamed *The Ryde Queen* after she was converted into a bar and restaurant.

A calm day on Wootton beach away from the hustle and bustle of the ferry terminal on the other side of Wootton Creek.

The copse is signposted with forest walks. A familiar sight in the early spring at the edge of the woodland is the bright yellow Brimstone butterfly, tempted out of hibernation by the warm weather. *Firestone Copse.*

The gates to the Royal Yacht Squadron's steps. The jetty is used by launches ferrying the club's members and VIPs from their boats.

Fireworks during Cowes Week. World famous for its yachting, Cowes fizzles with life during the Regatta in August.

His friend, Prince Philip, called him 'eccentric' - the two sailed regularly on the Prince's Flying Fifteen *Cowslip* and Uffa taught the young Royals to sail. Diana Harding, Uffa's great-niece, told me the story of how Uffa -took his revenge on a man who cycled along the public footpath every day near Twenty Acres, his home near The Folly at Whippingham. Uffa placed a rabbit he'd shot by the path and when the man appeared, shot out his front tyre. Uffa showed the outraged cyclist the dead rabbit and needless to say, the man never rode his bicycle that way again.

My bus journey ends at East Cowes where the chain ferry, or floating bridge, across the River Medina is already loading with cars. The spring tide is ebbing at 3-4 knots, there's a flukey wind and a tall-masted yacht sails past quickly. Years ago the local authority did a study on whether it would be feasible to build a bridge but nothing came of it and the floating bridge, one of the few still in use in the country, continues to clank back and forth across the river though its 'service frequency and crossing time depend on river traffic, tides and weather conditions'.

The shipyards on the Medina have always been famous – Queen Elizabeth 1 had *Rat of Wight*, a small sailing vessel made of oak from Parkhurst Forest, built at Cowes and men-of-war were being built in Nye's yard in 1696. Later the shipwrights' skills turned to aircraft like the seaplanes which were rolled down to the river on trolleys and to hovercraft, originally invented by Sir Christopher Cockerell and developed at Cowes.

Off the ferry and walking through Cowes, I remember the artist, Charles Raye, describing its streets in 1825 as being 'narrow and ill-built', a harsh description of a town that would become the Mecca of yachting and the home of the Royal Yacht Squadron, the most famous yacht club in the world. Part of the High Street has been modernised into a pedestrian precinct but the inside of the yacht chandler, Pascall Atkey founded in 1799 and one of the oldest in Britain, has hardly changed. The oldest part of the shop is built from ship's timbers and the shop is crammed from floor to ceiling with things that both dedicated 'yachties' and landlubbers alike enjoy.

The battery of 22 brass cannons in front of the Royal Yacht Squadron is used for the racing. The cannons came from the yacht, *Royal Adelaide*, and were presented to the Royal Yacht Squadron by Edward VII.

Passing a slipway off the High Street I catch glimpses of the harbour, hear the slap of water and the cries of gulls. Further along the street is 'The Prospect', an 1790 sail loft which the late Max Aitken restored and established as a small maritime museum with the help of friends. When the building was used as a sail loft, Ratsey and Lapthorn, the renowned sailmakers, made the mainsail for the yacht, *Britannia*, and now her sixty foot gaff hangs between the rafters of the museum. She was King George V's pride and joy and after he died in 1936, the yacht was towed out to sea with a garland of wild flowers on her foredeck and sunk in the waters off the Isle of Wight where she'd raced in her golden days. But she's not alone, *Meteor IV*, the last in a series of four yachts Kaiser Wilhelm 11 had built before the First World War to race against *Britannia*, was scuttled after her last owner died and lies near her rival.

It's all quiet on The Parade and the bronze cannons on the lower battlements of Cowes Castle are silent. Fired to signal the start of races in Cowes nine-day Regatta, the cannons are from William IV's yacht *Royal Adelaide*. They were used at Virginia Waters for the Royal Family's games until 1877 when Edward, Prince of Wales, presented them to the Squadron. Cowes Castle itself, and its twin at East Cowes, were built by Henry VIII in 1539 with stone he'd acquired from the recently dissolved religious houses of Beaulieu and Quarr. The castles' role was to defend the Island from invasion by the French and though soldiers were kept at Cowes Castle until the 19th century, the castle never fired a shot in anger.

Yachtsmen know, sometimes to their cost, about the rocky ledges that lurk beneath the sea between Cowes and Gurnard, but on my visit today the sea's on its best behaviour, spluttering up to the sea wall, then hissing back over a pebbled beach. Gurnard derives its name from the word 'gyran torr', meaning marshy shore, and Gurnard Marsh on a foggy day gives you the distinct feeling that Magwitch, the convict in Dickens' '*Great Expectations*' might be hiding there. Though a mooring-ring was found at an inland farm, over the centuries the harbour has silted up and the sea has swept away a Roman villa and a fort near where the River Luck runs into Gurnard Bay. Before the First World War Gurnard Regatta held a dog race where the animals were taken out in boats and launched overboard to race back to the shore. These days the rules are more lenient and now the dogs are allowed to wear lifejackets.

As Cowes gives way to the village of Gurnard, so Gurnard gives way to a rural countryside of farms and pastures, crumbling cliffs where mare's tail, a prehistoric-looking plant, sprouts from the clay and dainty goldfinches plunder teasel heads. I look at the map and follow the coastline to pick out my next

A place to sit and watch the world go by. The row of beach huts at Gurnard has a splendid view across the Solent to the entrance of the Beaulieu River and the New Forest.

The end of a day with dusk stealing over the sea at Gurnard. Although there's no proof that Gurnard was once part of the old tin-trail from Cornwall to Puckaster Cove, it's true that there's a warning sign for 'Toads in the Road!' in Rue Street.

Gurnard village and the sailing club. During the Cowes week this
part of the Solent is full of yachts racing.

Yachts moored in Cowes harbour. The town's High Street is full of
interesting shops and the Parade is a popular venue for watching
ships arriving or leaving Southampton.

From April to June the wood at Apesdown
has a white carpet of wild garlic, a plant
which thrives in the wood's moist
conditions.

CHAPTER TWO

Westward-Ho

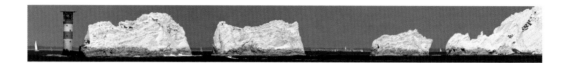

I drive through Porchfield to Newtown along lanes where the branches of the trees meet overhead with speckles of sunlight through the leaves and Mozart's Laudate Dominum playing on the radio. Newtown has always intrigued me. It's a place where I would like the 'real world' to fade momentarily and for a different one to be superimposed over it, as in a film flashback. For five or six seconds, it would be a summer's day in July 1256 and Newtown, or Frenchville, as the Bishop-elect of Winchester named his new town, would be celebrating the Feast of Mary Magdalen with a three-day fair.

Why a timeslip? Study a map of the area and you'll see that where once Newtown was a prosperous borough with a bustling market and a busy port trading in salt and oysters, these days it's a hamlet. Gold Street is a narrow field and the old High Street has turned into a grassy track. Gone are the merchants' houses though you can still see the boundaries to the small plots the burgesses rented for a shilling a year.

Newtown's prosperity began to decline with an outbreak of the Black Death, followed by the French raiding the village in 1377 and burning it to the ground. By the 1700s, only 12 of the houses were inhabited but Newtown was still sufficiently important to send two members to Parliament, a privilege granted by Elizabeth 1 until it was declared a Rotten Borough and disenfranchised in 1835.

But it's not entirely a ghost town. Noah's Ark has pride of place as the oldest house in the village - it was The Francheville Arms until the pub closed in 1916 and gets its name from the ark-like crest

Part of the land at Shalfleet bordering Newtown Estuary, this area was
purchased by the National Trust to preserve local wildlife.

Cranmore, with the arms of the trees stark against a
winter sky. Between here and Bouldnor, the woods
are home to some of the red squirrels on the Island.

Birds are attracted here by an abundance of shellfish and worms left on
the marshes by the receding tide. *Shalfleet Estuary.*

above the door - and the National Trust's Visitor Point has information and guides to the nature reserve on Newtown River. A hide on the marshes gives a 'bird's-eye' view of Shalfleet estuary, a delight for 'twitchers' or people like myself with a limited bird recognition. Follow a narrow footbridge over the marshes to the quay and the old salt-pans or wander through meadows where butterflies flit, safe from pesticides, among the wild flowers. While the National Trust doesn't encourage hordes of visitors to the site, the wardens are only too willing to give talks to schools or organisations.

And past the Visitors' Point, Newtown's 18th century Town Hall stands aloof from the rest of the village on a neat green plot. The wind moans round the building, a grandfather clock ticks solemnly in one corner of a room and the basement walls are covered with copies of ancient documents relating to its history. The hall was almost a ruin when Ferguson's Gang bought it for £5.00 and paid for the building to be restored in 1933 for the National Trust. The gang was made up of a group of eccentric benefactors who rescued threatened buildings in the 1930s and went under wonderful names like Sister Agatha, Shot Biddy, The Nark, Silent O'Moyle, Erb the Smasher, Wif the Artichoke and the Bludy Bishop. It was real cloak and dagger stuff with the money in Victorian coins being delivered by a masked messenger to the rather startled secretary of the National Trust.

An interesting item in the Town Hall's collection is a replica of the town's Henry VII silver-gilt mace, carved on one side with the king's arms and on its obverse, with the arms of the Commonwealth. The change in the carvings came about during the Civil War when the town's crafty burgesses decided that it was safer to 'hedge one's bets' and pledge allegiance to whoever was in power. The real mace, which previously belonged to the Simeon Family, is now on display at Carisbrooke Castle Museum.

Before leaving the hall I pause to take in the view from the top of the steps. Across the fields Causeway Lake shimmers in the sun, black headed gulls wheel and cry and somewhere over there is Cranmore and a scheme dreamt up in 1898 by a William Carter who planned to develop 375 acres of land into 168 small holdings and house plots at Cranmore Farm near the Newtown River. You could say William's idea fell on barren ground for the soil at Cranmore Park Estate was poor. Would-be buyers among the men returning home from the First World War found the Canadian government's offer of 160 acres of free land more attractive and by 1939 only 90 houses had been erected.

The Isle of Wight is one of the few places in Britain where red squirrels are found and the woods between Cranmore and Bouldnor are 'red squirrel territory'. But every now and then, there's a hue and cry on the Island when an aggressive grey squirrel, the red's natural enemy, is seen leaping from tree to tree or found squashed on the road. There's a possible answer to these false alarms. When the red squirrel, or *sciurus vulgaris* (from the Greek word 'skioros' meaning 'shade-tail') moults, its fur changes colour and sometimes it can be mistaken for a grey.

Squirrels, like humans, can be either right or left handed and these canny creatures don't waste valuable time opening dud nuts - they can tell by the weight of a hazel nut whether or not it contains a juicy kernel – facts I gleaned from Helen Butler, manager of the Wight Squirrel Project which collates information about the red squirrel population on the Island.

It was a Mr. Brocklehurst who, in 1876, released a pair of American grey squirrels into Henbury Park in Cheshire. So far the narrow strip of water which separates the Island from the mainland has stopped them invading the reds' territory and the Wight Squirrel Project has introduced rope walks and food hoppers to encourage the squirrels to cross safely if their wood has been fragmented by a busy road.

As I stop at the traffic lights in Shalfleet, I think of the old rhyme,

"Shalfleet poor and simple people
they sold their bells to buy a steeple."

Approaching Yarmouth from the east with the pier silhouetted against a sunset. At Cliff End there's barely a mile of water between the Isle of Wight and Hurst Castle.

Sentinel pine trees at Bouldnor Copse. Part of the Hamstead Heritage Coast, areas like this are still unspoilt compared to much of the mainland.

Engraved on the planks of Yarmouth's 609 ft. long walkway, the last remaining wooden operating pier in the British Isles, are the names of individuals and organisations who subscribed money towards the pier's restoration in the 1980s.

Hazel Hann, who lived at Brook Cottage by the Caul Bourne, prefers the village saying, 'Unless you fall in the brook, you aren't a Shalfleeter'. She remembers picking primroses and moss in the woods near the village to decorate the church at Easter and an evangelist arriving every year to set up a marquee in Withy Field behind the chapel. "We'd all sing hymns at the meeting," Hazel said, "and another thing we children loved, was the hurdy-gurdy man coming to the village. He was called Antonio and had a monkey on his shoulder and after he'd played a tune, we'd give him a penny or a halfpenny."

The road from Shalfleet leads to Yarmouth and as you approach the town from the east and look towards the pier, the Solent is busy with boats of all sizes. In the midst of them, the ferry plies back and forth from Lymington. This is the narrowest point to the mainland with barely a mile of water between Cliff End and Hurst Castle.

The shortness of the crossing made Yarmouth a handy place for Baldwin de Redvers, Earl of Devon and Lord of the Isle of Wight to stop en route to, or from his estates in Devon. Perhaps that's why he granted Yarmouth a royal charter in 1135 as it was the first town on the Island to receive this honour. That's the plus side of the town's history, the downside was its position – Yarmouth used to be almost surrounded by the sea which hindered its growth - and the French raids on the town in 1377 and 1524.

Its fortunes picked up after Newtown was destroyed by the French and Yarmouth's port became essential for the west side of the Island. The red-brick Town Hall in Yarmouth's square has a crest with a three-masted ship (one up on Newtown's two-master) and the words *'S.Commu. H.G. de Eremue'*, meaning the Common Seal of the Borough of Yarmouth. Nearby stands a 17th century building called Jireh House. There's The Bugle Coaching Inn, Harwoods, ironmongers and chandlers, who stock buckets, spades and windmills for those who prefer the gentler pursuits of childhood and the delicatessen across the square sells 'hand raised pork pies'.

I can't resist taking a saunter up the pier to study the names on the 552 deck planks. In 1980 when the pier, a Grade II Listed Building and the last remaining wooden operating pier in the British Isles, was in urgent need of restoration, the Harbour Commissioners launched a scheme to raise funds for the 609 ft.-long walkway famous for its attractive lattice-work handrails. The idea was for subscribers to have their names engraved on the planks and I find they vary from my favourites, 'The Owl and the Pussycat', and the Yarmouth Brownies to the *Bournemouth Belle*, a pleasure cruiser which called in at the pier.

I walk to the end of the pier where the sea slaps and gurgles round the new piles made of Greenheart, a South American hardwood immune from attack by a kind of seafaring woodworm called Gribble, and join a queue for a trip on the *Waverley*, a grand old lady and the only operational sea-going paddle steamer in the world. The sea is choppy but the *Waverley*, her paddles beating a comforting rhythm, sails sedately along the coast to the Needles at the tip of the Island. These colossal natural sculptures get their name from a 120 foot needle-shaped pinnacle called Lot's Wife which stood between the second and third rock until 1764 when it fell into the sea with a loud crump, a noise that was heard as far away as Portsmouth.

Sailing between the remaining stacks is known locally as 'Threading the Needle' and when 'H.M.S. Assurance' was returning home in 1782 with the Governor of Jamaica on board, the ship's master boasted to his important passanger that he could sail the ship close to the Needles "so close that the fly of the ensign might touch the rock." Minutes later the ship struck Goose Rock near the Needles stacks and sank. Fortunately, none of the crew lost their lives and the governor managed to save the £60,000 fortune he had brought home. In 1859 the Needles lighthouse came into operation and stands, painted in a barber's pole colours of red and white, on a rock platform at the seaward end.

Back on terra firma, I feel I can't leave Yarmouth without tracking down Sir Robert Holmes, or rather his statue, in the church of St. James. Sir Robert was Governor of the Island for 24 years and

The colossal chalk stacks at the tip of the Island got their name from a needle-shaped pinnacle called Lot's Wife which stood between the second and third rock until it fell into the sea in 1764.

Looking at the Needles from sea level. The lighthouse came into operation in 1859 and stands on a rock platform.

being Yarmouth's most famous inhabitant, has his own chapel. I can only describe the expression on the statue's face as 'miffed' and the head a trifle too big for the body. But the reason for this becomes clear when I read the accompanying text. Robert captured a French vessel with a faceless statue onboard meant to be of King Louis XIV of France. The governor then ordered the sculptor, who was also captured, to put his own, Robert's face on it.

Holmes's residence was the present-day George Hotel where the staircase that Charles 11 used when he visited in July 1671 still exists. But the tradition of celebrating St. James's Day on 25 July has lapsed. It was a day when the townspeople could celebrate and not fall foul of the law - an unique custom announced by an official sticking a stuffed glove on the end of a rod out of an upstairs window in the town hall.

I wander through one of the little alleys that lead to the harbour where the *RNLB Eric and Susan Hiscock (Wanderer)* is moored alongside the quay. The castle, another of Henry VIII's fortifications

Gorse in bloom on Headon Warren with a view beyond of Alum Bay and the Needles.

against the French, watches benignly as a sleek cruiser glides into the harbour rocking the yachts on their moorings. Further along the quay is the sand house, now part of a boatbuilding yard, but previously used to store fine white sand from Hatherwood Point before it was shipped on to London and Bristol for glassmaking in the 18th century.

More famous by far are Alum Bay's coloured sands, so it seems sensible to get aboard the open-topped bus waiting at The Needles Park for a trip to the Needles Old Battery and a good view of the cliffs. As the bus climbs the steep road, I look back to the bay and the cliffs streaked with ochre, grey, black, yellow and red – the five most popular colours of the 20 multi-coloured bands. Because the rocks were laid down at different times their age ranges from 35 million years old to 65 million years old. Small clouds cast dark blue shadows on the sea and there's a popple of white foam on the Bridge Roll, the shingle bank in the middle of the Needles Channel. England and the New Forest look almost touchable from here.

The bus stops at the top and I hurry down the steps to the Old Battery – another of Lord Palmerston's fortifications - to see two 1874 bulbous-shaped guns which, a notice tells me, needed nine men to load and fire each one. The guns were thrown off the cliff into the sea and then rescued later which strikes me as rather odd. I walk to the edge of the headland from where, the splendid sunsets are second only to those in the Bay of Mexico. On my way out I avoid descending a spiral staircase to a claustrophobic-looking underground tunnel and catch the bus back to civilization.

Headon Down is tinged with purple heather as I drive to Farringford House to seek out the tree that Guiseppe Garibaldi planted when he visited the Poet Laureate, Alfred Lord Tennyson, and his wife, Emily, at their "ivied house among the pine trees" in 1864. Sadly, although I find it, the tree is bare and sticks out of the shrubbery like a telegraph pole. But the inside of the house, now an hotel, is a delight with its Victorian atmosphere. I linger long enough to see Tennyson's bedroom and his study with a spiral staircase he used for a hasty exit if he heard unwelcome visitors about to descend on him.

At the edge of the grounds, a gate leads east to Freshwater Bay which Tennyson used when he visited his neighbour, the photographer Julia Margaret Cameron at her home in Dimbola Lodge, named after a tea plantation in Ceylon. It was a gift of a camera in 1863 after she came to live on the Island that sparked off Julia Margaret Cameron's enthusiasm for photography. She converted a chicken-house into a studio, a coal-house into a dark room and photographed famous Victorians like Darwin, Edward Lear, the actress Ellen Terry and Tennyson who said he especially liked her photograph of him called 'The Dirty Monk'. But though Cameron's stay at Freshwater had been a whirlwind of activity, in 1875 and at the height of her fame, she and her family returned to Ceylon with their worldly goods packed in coffins (a necessary provision for the long sea voyage.)

One of Tennyson's favourite walks was over the down that bears his name and where today a marble Celtic cross stands, erected in his memory by the people of Freshwater on the site of the old beacon. Whatever the weather he would stride across the springy sheep-cropped turf, his cloak

A sketch by J.M.W. Turner shows fishermen busy at their nets in Totland Bay where Trinity House pilot vessels used to berth at the pier. But Totland Bay's sandy beach remains a popular place for visitors to the west coast of the Island.

Creamy waves breaking on the beach with Alum Bay
and the Needles in the background.

Parasenders chasing the thermals above Alum Bay.

billowing in the wind, reciting aloud lines from his poems like 'The Charge of the Light Brigade'. Here, Tennyson claimed, "the air was worth sixpence a pint."

I drive past St. Agnes Church, built on land given by Tennyson and the only thatched church on the Island. Dave Woodford, whose family were thatchers on the Island for four generations, used water reed from the River Yar for rethatching the roof. The river flows through marshes the other side of Freshwater Bay to the Causeway and on to Yarmouth and on a bright winter's morning when the marsh reeds are frosted like sugar icing, a magical sight. Near the Causeway is a seat dedicated to the memory of Captain Rory O'Conor who lost his life when the ship under his command, *HMS Neptune*, sank in the Mediterranean in 1941. The best time to visit Freshwater Bay is in a howling gale when the sea is seriously rough and huge waves crash on the shore. High on the headland above the bay stands Fort Redoubt, built in the mid-nineteenth century. The gunners stationed there used the ranging mark off Hanover Point for firing practice.

The combined efforts of sea and wind did for Arch Rock in 1992 when the arch, once a local landmark, collapsed. Stag Rock stands fair and square in the bay and according to a local legend, gets its name from a deer who leapt from the cliffs on to the rock to escape from Lord Holmes' hounds. Here's another tit-bit about his lordship – he's reputed to have used the caves at the foot of the cliffs for entertaining his guests with the wine cooled in a cave called *Lord Holmes Cellar,* food prepared in *Lord Holmes Kitchen,* and high jinks in *Lord Holmes Parlour.*

And thinking of entertainment, in 1970 there was the Isle of Wight Pop Festival at nearby Afton. It caused a lot of controversy at the time but this is an extract from Brian Hinton's *"Message of Love"*, an account of the event.

"The festival provided an alternative society. A society where people forgot their particular class, creed, race or religion and were able to live together and do the simple things of life on a friendly basis. There's something in that, I'm sure. Think about it."

Sunlight changes the cliffs to gold in Freshwater Bay. Stag Rock gets its name from a deer that escaped from the hounds by leaping on to the rock.

The marble Celtic cross was erected in memory of the poet, Alfred Lord Tennyson, by the people of Freshwater on the downs where he said the air was "worth sixpence a pint."

Afton Marsh in the late afternoon. St. Agnes' church at Freshwater was rethatched using local water reed.

CHAPTER THREE

Fossils, Wrecks and Smugglers

The road over Afton Down curves to the bottom of the hill, then climbs to where I look down on Compton Bay and a sea that's almost Mediterranean blue. Millions of years ago when the Island was joined to southern England, it was covered with water. Layers of Wealden, Lower Greensand, Gault, Upper Greensand and chalk were deposited on the area we call the Isle of Wight as the Island sank and rose again. It seems blue slipper clay is the villian, causing everything to slip and slide. But in the geologists' book – terrific. Nowhere else in England, they say, that's equal in size to the Island, is more interesting.

I've come to the south western coast of the Island where fossil dinosaur remains lurk in the Wealden clay at Compton Bay, Blackgang Chine is formed from Lower Greensand and the Undercliff from Upper Greensand. Here deep freshwater ravines, called chines, a local word of Saxon origin, bisect the cliff-line and a colony of European butterflies, the Glanville Fritillaries *(Melitaea cinxia)*, unknown elsewhere in the British Isles, flourishes. So it's not surprising that this part of the Island's coastline has been designated as a Site of special Scientific interest.

The coffee-brown cliffs are fossil-rich and there's a cormorant perched on Fort Redoubt's leading mark. It's low tide so I walk carefully over a seaweed-covered rock shelf at Hanover Point to look for a trail of footprints left by a young 20 foot tall iguanadon. Where I stand would have been a muddy flood plain 115 million years ago and lying in a pool nearby, is the iguanadon's larder – toppled pieces of fossilised giant conifer tree trunks which the dinosaurs found tasty. The beach is

Compton Bay has one of the best beaches on the Island. It's also popular with windsurfers and when the tide recedes, with fossil hunters searching for treasures from the past.

a treasure-trove of fossilised bits of its spiky foliage, ballast from sunken ships, pieces of fool's gold and beneath the cliff face I discover what looks like a lump of chalk but is a cast of a iguanodon's three-toed footprint half-buried in the sand. When the river flooded it filled the animal's muddy footprints with sand which set like concrete.

In addition to its geological and fossil interest, this stretch of coast is famous for the notorious Atherfield Ledge, a 'lee-shore' graveyard for sailing ships like the three-masted *S.V. Sirenia* which drifted off course on a foggy March day in 1888 and ran aground in heavy seas. Although there was no wind, the waves were hitting the reef with a thunderous boom and roaring on to the shore. The crew of the Brook lifeboat, *Worcester Cadet,* managed to reach the stricken vessel to take off the captain's wife and children and two other people but on its second attempt, the lifeboat capsized and the Coxswain, Moses Munt, the Second Coxswain, Tom Cotton, and two of the ship's crew were drowned.

Worse was to come. The Brook lifeboat *William Slaney Lewis* had also been launched but after rowing six miles through terrible seas, a huge icy wave broke over the lifeboat and three of the crew were washed overboard. Two were saved but the Second Coxswain, Reuben Cooper, was swept away. After searching in vain for Reuben, the remaining crew were forced to anchor until morning when a last effort was made to reach the wreck but by then they were exhausted and had to return to Brook. The Brighstone lifeboat finally managed to rescue the remainder of the *Sirenia's* crew and bring them ashore.

I did a detour to Brook village to see the boards in the church of St. Mary the Virgin commemorating the lifeboat's service. It's an impressive record, the first lifeboat aptly called *Dauntless* was launched in 1860 and she and her successors together saved 263 lives; the crews at the Brighstone station saved 433 lives and the Atherfield lifeboats saved 157 people. Today these stations are no longer in service. Instead, the R.N.L.I brought in more powerful boats at Yarmouth and Bembridge. No wonder Chale Bay because of its terrible history was called 'The Graveyard' or 'The Bay of Death'.

Looking west from Mottistone Down. The Down is well-known for its Long Stone, a Neolithic 14ft. tall monolith which stands at the top.

These were hard times when men earned barely enough to support a family so when a ship's cargo was washed ashore, the local people didn't miss a chance for salvage. In 1882, a steamship called the *Wheatfield* was wrecked at Blackgang Point, and news soon got around that there were bags of flour and tins of beef for the taking. The wreck was remembered fondly afterwards as 'the flour ship'.

In 1314 when Walter de Godeton, a Lord of the Manor, claimed a cargo of wine washed ashore from the wreck of the *Ship of Blessed Mary*, he was taken to court and fined for unlawfully salvaging the wine. But according to chroniclers that wasn't the end of the story. The casks of wine had come from a monastery in Picardy and the Church threatened him with excommunication unless he built a lighthouse on *Montem de Cheal*, Chale Mountain, with a chapel for a priest to sing masses for the souls of the dead.

I leave the car to cross the road, clamber over a stile and start to climb to St. Catherine's Oratory, known locally as The Pepper Pot. It is a bit of a slog but the view at the top seduces the senses: this is one of the best places to see the sixty-mile Round the Island race in June when the yachts have their multi-coloured spinnackers up. Country lanes wander among a patchwork of fields and the hillsides are dotted with woodland, to the west are the white chalk cliffs at Freshwater Bay and in the far distance, the Dorset coast. There's the Military Road from Chale to Freshwater, built originally for the swift deployment of troops in Palmerston's time. In 1933 the track was made into a coastal road using unemployed men for labour, but, if you look carefully, you may spot one of the old helmet-topped hollow posts that marked the track. To the north of where I stand is the Hoy monument, a tall pillar erected by a Russian merchant called Michael Hoy to commemorate a visit to Britain in 1814 by Czar Alexander.

But I'm here to see Godeton's medieval lighthouse, the second oldest to survive in Britain and looking every bit like a stone space rocket poised for liftoff with its octagonal tower and conical nose cone roof. For over 200 years the lamp in the tower sent out comforting rays of light to mariners at sea but in 1547 when Henry VIII ordered the dissolution of chantries, the chapel to the east of the building was vandalised and the stone robbed for building, so that today only the lighthouse tower exists.

Called The Pepper Pot because of its shape, St. Catherine's Oratory is a medieval lighthouse, built by Walter de Godeton some say, as an act of penance for trying to steal a cargo of wine from a shipwreck.

This tall column was raised in 1814 by Michael Hoy to commemorate a visit by Tsar Alexander 1 of Russia. Ironically, it was rededicated in 1857 in honour of men killed at the Siege of Sevastopol fighting those same Russians.

The ideal time for a walk on St. Catherine's Down is at bluebell time during April and May.

The 86 ft. tall St. Catherine's lighthouse was lit by oil lamps until 1887. Today its revolving white light has a range of 26 miles, flashing every five seconds to warn shipping.

Looking across a field of buttercups to St. Catherine's lighthouse. It came into operation on 23 March, 1840 and in 1943, three of the keepers were killed in a hit-and-run attack by a German plane.

Nearby is a squat building surrounded by a wire fence, an abortive attempt by Trinity House to build a lighthouse and dubbed The Salt Pot or The Mustard Pot. The present lighthouse on St. Catherine's Point came into operation on 23 March, 1840, but the 120 ft. tower was often hidden by heavy sea mists and in 1875 its height was reduced to 86 ft. Lit by oil lamps until 1887, it has a revolving white light with a range of 26 miles flashing every 5 seconds to warn vessels of the dangers of the Race when the tides are running fast. When a thick sea mist creeps in from the sea, the foghorn's mournful bellow can be heard for miles around.

This area called 'Back of Wight' is also well-known for the smuggling that took place in the past. The poet, Sidney Dobell commented, "Here are fishermen who never fish, but always have pockets full of money; and farmers whose farming consists in 'ploughing the deep' by night, and whose daily time is spent in standing, like herons, on look-out posts."

It's easy to romanticize the facts, to remember Rudyard Kipling's poem, *A Smuggler's Song*, and to think of the Excisemen as 'the baddies'. Imagine the thrill the smugglers must have felt when they managed to outrun a Revenue pilot cutter and land the contraband without being caught by a coastguard's patrol. When the wind and tide were right for a trip to Barfleur or Cherbourg, the smugglers would spread a story about a ghostly 'flying hare' at Brighstone to keep people indoors; flat-topped tombs in churchyards were used to hide the caches of brandy-tubs, sometimes it was a pigsty, an underground cellar or a hayrick.

In the 18th century a labourer earned as little as ten shillings a week and beachcombing, wrecking and smuggling were part of Island life. Despite the penalty for smuggling being severe - a man could be sentenced to six months in jail or shipped off to serve on a man-o'-war - the high duties on imported brandy, tea, tobacco, silk and lace made trips across the Channel worth the risk and the extra money handy.

The busy months were between May and September when the fishing boats wouldn't be missed and the fishermen moonlighted as smugglers. The local squire and parson would put up the cash for the run while the shore gang would be responsible for landing the cargo and distributing it. Driving along the Military Road where the trees and hedges are slanted against the south-westerly winds, I make a note to go to Brighstone another day to search for a cottage where the chalk blocks in the walls are carved with silhouettes of ships, reputed to be secret messages from smugglers.

Brighstone is also famous for William Fox, a fossil fanatic and a curate at the village church in Victorian times. William made several important discoveries including a sort of reptilian hedgehog, *Polacanthus foxii*. But his enthusiasm for dinosaurs did not go down well with his parishioners who complained he was more interested in bones than the church.

Away from the coast, there's a dramatic change in the scenery. I drive through the Undercliff which sags towards the sea between Luccombe and Blackgang Chine, a landfall covered with trees, tangles of ivy and wild clematis and an undergrowth of briars and ferns – what you might call 'Nature's gloryhole' or an island within an island. It's pretty unique as there are only two other places like this in Britain and the untamed Undercliff was pure manna for Victorian writers, poets and artists like J.M.W. Turner who painted the view from the terrace of The Orchards, one of the rather fine houses built on the south side of the road.

Not far from the road is the church of St. Lawrence-under-Wath, built in the 12th century and the smallest church in England until a chancel was added in 1842. You'll see the door in the north wall has been blocked up because a rector, hurrying to take a service in the church in the 18th century, hit his head on the lintel of the door and subsequently died from his injuries.

The Island's microclimate prompted a Dr. James Clark to describe it as, 'the British Madeira' in his book, *'The Influence of Climate in the Prevention and Cure of Chronic Diseases'*, published in 1829.

A typical Isle of Wight downland scene.
The gate invites you to follow
the trail to West Wight.
St. Catherine's Down

Freshwater ravines called *chines* (a local word of Anglo-Saxon origin) bisect the southwestern cliff-line of the Island. Whale Chine's deep canyon is probably the most impressive.

Though there's no proof that the monks of Lyre founded Bonchurch Old Church in the eighth century, a visit to the little church dedicated to St. Boniface shouldn't be missed.

Brighstone village nestles against the downs. One of Brighstone's famous inhabitant's was the Rev. William Fox, a fossil fanatic who discovered the *Polacanthus foxii*, a sort of reptilian hedgehog.

And forty years later, here on the south coast of the Island, the quarter-of-a-mile-long Royal National Hospital for Diseases of the Chest was opened, founded by a physician and naturalist called Arthur Hill Hassall who had suffered from tuberculosis and convalesced at Ventnor. Patients from all over Britain were treated at the hospital for tuberculosis and other chest complaints until the arrival of antibiotics made it redundant and it closed in 1964.

I drive into Ventnor and think how Arthur Hill Hassall would have been delighted at the Local Authority refusal to allow the site to be developed. They chose instead to create a garden whose philosophy today is to "provide a public amenity that can be used for recreation, education and conservation." The late Sir Harold Hillier was involved in the design and the 22 acre garden, opened by Earl Mountbatten in 1972, has kept paths and lawns from the old Victorian garden, sunny walls where peaches and nectarines ripened and a fig tree that's more than 100 years old.

I park the car in Ventnor Botanic Garden. As demolition work started on the old hospital buildings, men working in the operating theatre smelt whiffs of ether and saw a ghostly figure. Those were the stories but hundreds of patients were treated in the 96 years the hospital was open, enjoying a return-to-health regime of rest and healthy food in the Island's mild climate, a treatment almost unheard of in 1869. As the patients' health improved, they helped to look after the poultry and grow fruit and vegetables for the hospital's needs. There's a photograph of a line of men in the garden, each carrying a trug (it was the hospital's policy to separate the sexes when they worked in the grounds.) Fortunately, the stained Pre-Raphaelite and Art Nouveau glass windows in the chapel were saved and installed in the parish church of St. Lawrence.

I saw the garden when the terrible storm of October 1987 destroyed nearly 500 trees. Now it's been replanted with a variety of trees, shrubs and plants, some so tender they can only grow in a climate similar to the Undercliff. Difficult areas, like the steep bank beside the Dr. Henry Behrend Walk, have been terraced using timber from Ventnor Pier when it was demolished. The theme of the

Green House, opened in 1987, is to show how plants cover up mankind's effect on the landscape, such as old mining works. One of the exhibits is an ancient variety of fern called Selaginella which used to grow on tropical parts of the earth 60 million years ago. The plant is particularly interesting as Ventnor Botanic Garden have a sandstone slab with a fossilised fern inside it, exactly the same as the one growing in the Green House.

I resume my drive round the south-west coast of the Island, dipping down into Ventnor with its steep and winding streets. The town lies beneath St. Boniface Down, the highest spot on the Island, and, in Queen Victoria's time Ventnor was one of the most fashionable holiday spots in Europe. Dickens came here and so did Turgenev, who was inspired to write *'Fathers and Sons'* when he stayed at Belinda Cottage. "This island is a little gem," wrote Karl Marx in a letter to his friend Friedrich Engels in 1874; Marx spent his last two winters in Ventnor before he died.

The town is built on terraces, a mish-mash of houses "in every conceivable style and every outrageous shape," complained the Reverend E. Venables, writing about the Isle of Wight in 1860. I like the look of the Victorian villas I pass but driving down the steep Zig Zag Road needs all my concentration and I park in the centre of Ventnor where everything is within easy reach.

I stroll past an array of interesting antique shops and small cafés to Pier Street and down to the Esplanade where a stream that once served a watermill on the cliff, flows through the Cascade Gardens, designed by Edgar J. Harvey around 1900. Ventnor's original pier had a 100 ft. gap cut in it during the war to stop it being used as a landing point and the town suffered heavily from raids because of the early warning radar station on the top of St. Boniface Down. It had been built early in 1939 to detect enemy aircraft approaching the Island and after one raid Lord Haw Haw was heard on the radio announcing "a great German victory of military targets on the south coast of the Isle of Wight."

Ventnor's Cascade Gardens were designed around 1900 by Edgar J. Harvey, the town's surveyor for 19 years.

Wander along the shore at Steephill Cove, a small roadless seashore hamlet, to recapture an image of summers past.

Ventnor's houses cluster on terraces beneath St. Boniface Down with zig-zagging roads leading to the High Street and the Promenade.

Returning to Pier Street I hurry back to the car as I want to have a look at Bonchurch, 'the leafy part of Ventnor'. This is another place where the inhabitants were involved in smuggling and all sorts of shenanigans, like frightening people with a phantom coach and horseman by padding the horse's hooves and dabbing phosphorus on the rider. It's also full of literary associations as the poet, Algernon Charles Swinburne, spent his childhood at East Dene and is buried in the local church of St. Boniface, worth a visit if only to see Joan Wolfenden's tapestries. The ozier pond in the village, which provided material for the local fishermen's lobster pots, was given to the village by the writer, H. de Vere Stacpoole, in memory of his wife. Though Stacpoole is often remembered for 'The Blue Lagoon', he also wrote 'Of Mice and Men', a book about his life in Bonchurch.

I drive past the pond and up the twists and turns of Bonchurch Shute and Winterbourne where Charles Dickens stayed in 1849 while he wrote *David Copperfield* and out on to the main road at the top. Below me, I leave Ventnor basking in the sun – one of the Island's Victorian gems.

Blue skies and bluebells on the downs above Ventnor. It's spring and there's a promise of summer in the air.

CHAPTER FOUR

Beside the Seaside

The dip in British seaside holidays began in the late 1950s and in Ventnor's case, the town wasn't helped by the railway line being axed in 1953. Luckily the neighbouring towns of Shanklin and Sandown escaped the cuts and visitors can still reach these seaside resorts by rail.

Driving east from Ventnor I come to Shanklin Old Village, a collection of thatched cottages, curiosity shops and the Crab Inn, to follow up a hint from the poet, John Keats, who stayed in the village in 1819 and talked of a "wondrous Chine". He was, of course, referring to Shanklin Chine, a deep gash in the cliff with overhanging trees and tinkling waterfalls, rare plants and wildlife and the Island's first tourist attraction when it was opened to the public by a William Colenutt in 1817.

I wander along the paths William cut beside a stream and linger on a rustic bridge where the Victorian visitors must have 'oohed' and 'aahed' over the Chine's wild beauty though it was probably lost on the men of the 40 Royal Marine Commados when they trained here in 1942 for the Dieppe raid. There's a Memorial to them near the Chine's Heritage Centre where I satisfy my curiosity about PLUTO (Pipeline under the Ocean), the brainchild of Lord Mountbatten. Pluto, a forked pipeline from Shanklin Chine and Sandown, stretched 65 miles under the Channel and during the Normandy invasion, carried millions of gallons of fuel to France.

William Colenutt must have had an eye for business because besides opening the Chine to the public, he was the first person to put a bathing machine on the beach. But he wasn't the only

Colourful beach huts under the cliff face at Shanklin.

A view from Shanklin Down with the sweep of Sandown Bay and
Culver's white cliffs in the distance.

entrepreneur in the family - in 1845 his son-in-law James Sampson hit on the idea of providing visitors with hot brine baths by heating the sea water in a copper boiler.

Shanklin was one of the places on the Island blessed, depending how you felt when you tasted chalybeate or iron water, with mineral springs. Publicity about the springs and their high iron content persuaded foreign visitors to desert the spas in Germany and flock to Shanklin and in 1900 the Royal Spa Hotel went up-market from providing a drink from a spring in a grotto to a suite of chalybeate hot and cold baths.

What really led to the town's expansion was the arrival in 1864 of a train service from Ryde to Shanklin. Before that, travel between the two towns had been by coach and four which went under the wonderful name of 'Surprise', a journey which took two and a half hours but with the coming of the train, flocks of visitors began to arrive. And when the pier opened in 1891, steamers started to call regularly to pick up passengers for trips around the Island or to places like Bournemouth and Weymouth. Sadly, the pier was destroyed by the Great Storm in 1987.

I leave Shanklin and drive to Sandown to take a look at a red post box in Melville Street, one of the few emblazoned with 'Edward VIII', the king who was never crowned. The seaside resort of Sandown became popular in the mid 19th century when its gently sloping sandy sheltered bay attracted Victorian visitors including Lewis Carroll who loved Sandown Originally a small fishing village, Sandown, or Sandham, developed as a garrison town when Henry VIII built a castle near the shore in 1537. It was the first of three forts, two succumbed as the sea undermined the foundations and the present fort which was built in 1866 is now a zoo.

Along Culver Parade I pass Dinosaur Isle, a museum shaped like a giant pterosaur and the place to check out dinosaur history on the Island, and on through Yaverland and turn up the steep road to the top of Bembridge Down, passing the Palmerston fort snuggled into the side of the hill. Lord

Yarborough, the first Commodore of the Royal Yacht Squadron, has a fine monument to his memory on the headland and I stand there, looking south over Sandown Bay, then turning to look north at the view over Whitecliff Bay and on to Bembridge harbour.

The headland ends in Culver Cliff, a sheer drop to the sea. Its name comes from the Anglo-Saxon word *culfre*, meaning dove or pigeon and in the 1950s a small Iron Age sandstone Janus head was discovered on the cliff. According to archaeologists it was from a fairly well-known head cult in Celtic Europe whose adherents made a habit of chopping off peoples' heads. Nasty.

Before I reach Bembridge I pull off the road and stop by the sign to Centurion's Copse. Ernest Du Boulay in his book, *Bembridge Past and Present*, published in 1911, calls it 'St. Urian's Copse' and talks of a chapel dedicated to the saint which used to stand to the left of Pilgrims Lane, a narrow lane leading down to the copse. The pebbly path has high hedges on either side and away from the main road, I suddenly realise there are no birds are singing and the old legends I've heard about the wood spring to mind. Like many tales from the past they vary, but all agree on one thing – that once a town called Wolverton existed on the banks of Brading Haven, the big estuary which used to cover Sandown marshes and the Yar valley, and that the town was destroyed by the French around 1340.

The story about a hermit who lived on Culver Cliff varies – some versions say he'd told the townspeople that as long as the well at St. Urian's chapel remained pure, Wolverton would continue to thrive. Unfortunately, a visiting pilgrim, completely unaware of the prophesy, touched the well with a palm frond and was stoned to death for tainting it. Another version says the hermit rushed down the hill to tell the people in the town that the French were coming but nobody believed him. Whichever story you believe, it's true that Wolverton was burnt to the ground and completely destroyed.

According to Boulay, stones from the chapel were taken and built into Yaverland church and the wood's name changed from St. Urian's to Centurions when Roman artefacts were discovered nearby.

Looking towards Culver Cliff from Yaverland. The name Culver comes from the Anglo-Saxon word *culfre*, meaning a dove or pigeon.

Park the car on Brading Down and you'll have a superb view over the Island. It's a place for a picnic or an ice cream and a visit to Brading Roman Villa at the foot of the down, built with a sedum roof to harmonize with the surrounding countryside.

Wild daffodils in Centurion's Copse. Originally known as St. Urian's Copse, it was here that the French destroyed the village of Wolverton around 1340.

It's a spooky place, dark and damp-smelling under the trees but I want to find the old wall which protected Woverton in the days when the sea covered the flat land between Sandown and Culver Cliff as far as Brading, almost separating Bembridge from the rest of the Island.

In those days Brading was a busy port and ships sailed up to the town to moor at the quay where Charles II disembarked on his visit to Sandham Castle. I find the wall and walk to the edge of the wood and the marshes. Sometimes on a moonlit September night when a mist, called the White Lady, creeps in, I've been told it looks as though the sea has returned but today the rain has cleared and I can hear the water tumbling over a weir into the Eastern Yar which winds through the fields to Bembridge harbour. Back in the car I pass the aircraft factory where John Britten and Desmond Norman built the 'Islander', a light STOL aircraft designed in its early days as a rugged utility plane for the Third World countries. At the beginning of the last war trenches were dug across the airfield to stop enemy gliders from landing and it's here that enactments of the Schneider Trophy Air Race, though without seaplanes, have taken place.

As I emerge from Steyne Woods I can see Bembridge Windmill, a typical cap mill and the only windmill left standing on the Island. It was neglected after it stopped working in 1913 at the outbreak of the First World War and was used by the local Home Guard in the Second World War. Eventually the Isle of Wight National Trust Properties raised enough money to restore the windmill to full working order and transfer it into the care of the National Trust.

I step into a gloomy interior where the floor has been trodden by generations of millers and the smell of corn clings to the thick wooden beams. There are four floors in the windmill which still has much of its original machinery and on one floor I come across the part of the system which kept the grain running called The Damsel, called that because it's never silent but always chattering. An inscription, 'E BEKER 1746 A C', was discovered during recent restoration work on the wooden steps inside and means the windmill was probably in use before the land was reclaimed from Brading Haven. J.M.W. Turner's water colour of the mill in 1795 was painted during the day, but I like the windmill at sunset when its sails, or sweeps, are silhouetted against a sky of red and gold - magic.

Look at an old map and there, in the north-east of the Isle of Wight, is 'Binbridge Isle' or 'Yar Island', surrounded on the one side by sea and by the marshes and the Eastern Yar on the other. It's been suggested that Bembridge might have got its name from an early bridge, a 'beam-bridge' in Saxon times but on the old maps the little eastern isle is shown joined to Morton by a causeway built in 1388 by William Russell, Lord of Yaverland, after he drained some of the marshes.

Now Bembridge is a picturesque village set around a natural harbour and one of the largest parishes in the country. Oh, the remembered joy of travelling to Bembridge by train before Lord Beecham axed the line, known locally as the "crabby-winkle" line, in 1953. The excitement of a cow wandering across the two and half miles of track and the sound of the train's whistle as we rattled along to Bembridge station. We lingered to watch the engine on the turntable, then stepped outside the station to feel the air filled with salt tang from the harbour where houseboats of all shapes and sizes from barges to motor-torpedo gun boats were moored.

The houseboats are still there but the station has gone and so has the tollgate where you paid sixpence to British Rail for the privilege of using the road to St. Helens. When the railway was built in 1878, quays and railway sidings were constructed at St. Helens and I think a story about the vessel *P.S. Carrier,* which carried goods wagons between St. Helens and Langstone on the mainland, is worth a mention. The service wasn't profitable and didn't last for long but on the 50th anniversary of Queen Victoria's accession to the throne the *Carrier* was used for excursion trips when Queen Victoria was reviewing the Naval Fleet. The ship's brief claim to notoriety came when her captain committed the terrible *faux pas* of sailing ahead of the royal yacht and belching out thick black smoke

Where did I learn this gem? In the old school building near the church is the Bembridge Heritage Centre, manned by enthusiastic volunteers and full of interesting facts about the village's history. They also have one of the huge pumps used in the PLUTO operation on show.

The only windmill left standing on the Island, Bembridge windmill is a "Tower" or "Cap" mill. Used by the Home Guard during the Second World War, the mill was restored to full working order before being handed into the care of the National Trust.

St Helen's Old Church, a white-painted seamark in transit with another aide to navigation, Ashey Down.

A view across St. Helen's Bay to the old church. Sailors used stones from the ruined church to scour the ships' decks – hence the origin of the word "holystone".

Re-enactment of the Schneider Trophy Air Race. Originally the race was flown with seaplanes.

I leave the harbour where the Redwings, the oldest surviving keel boat class in Great Britain, are moored in line beyond Bembridge Sailing Club. Built for single-handed racing and with distinctive red sails, these craft are very much part of the Bembridge scene. At one time there was a pier next to the clubhouse for a ferry from Portsmouth to dock and at The Point nearby, villagers kept a cannon in Nelson's time to warn all the able bodied men in the village to hide before the pressgang arrived from the naval ships anchored in nearby St. Helen's Road.

Another Bembridge landmark is the lifeboat station so I drive up the hill, passing an unusual phone box in the High Street, a Post Office K1 design which dates from 1921 and is the last of its kind in southern England. I want to talk to Martin Woodward, who was Second Coxswain and then Coxswain on the Bembridge lifeboat until he retired after twenty years with the Royal National Lifeboat Institution. Martin, besides writing books and diving on wrecks, raises funds for the Isle of Wight Historic Lifeboat Trust which has already paid for the restoration of Queen Victoria, Bembridge's first lifeboat.

We sit in his house overlooking the sea and Martin tells me that since its restoration, the vintage lifeboat has been used for a recreation of the overland launch in 1877 when the boat was pulled six miles from Bembridge to Sandown to help rescue the crew of the *John Douse,* a brig which had gone aground late in the evening in Sandown Bay. Launched into the stormy sea, the lifeboat spent more than an hour in the dark searching for the brig and its crew who were clinging to the rigging. After rescuing the captain and mate, the Bembridge men spent a miserable night at sea until dawn when the coastguards were able to take off the rest of the crew.

"The other event we run to raise money for the Trust," says Martin, "is the annual re-enaction of Joey Attrill's fifteen-mile walk from Bembridge to Atherfield to help rescue the crew of the *Sirenia.*" Joey was awarded ten shillings (50p) by the Mayor of Newport for his efforts. "With courage, everything is possible," is the RNLI's motto, adopted in honour of Sir William Hillary, a remarkable far-seeing man who founded the 'Royal National Institution for the preservation of life from shipwreck' in 1824.

Afterwards I walk to the Bembridge lifeboat pier, built out on the edge of a ledge, where the 24-ton *Max Aitken III* is kept in the boathouse, ready to give assistance anywhere in its 120 square mile operational area. When a call comes through, the lifeboatmen are paged and following Bembridge tradition, two maroons fired. The crew run along the pier to the boathouse and the lifeboat is launched rapidly down a slipway into the sea. Until 1922, the boat was launched from the beach and six horses used to pull it back when it returned.

For centuries Island life has been entwined with the sea. St. Helen's Roads was a snug anchorage for ships waiting for the right wind to sail down-Channel and during the Napoleonic wars the people of St. Helens profited from selling meat, eggs and beer to the ships. Another thing which kept the pennies rolling in was the 'sweet water' from a spring Under Tyne, known for its special quality which somehow stopped it tasting salty after it had been kept in barrels for a long time at sea.

The view from Ashey Down over the Arreton valley to the south and the Solent and mainland to the north is spectacular. The white-painted triangular seamark was built as an aid to navigation in 1735.

Priory Bay looks peaceful but in the 18th century, it was a favourite place for smugglers like Dickie Dawes and it was here that his daughter, Sophie, fortune-hunter and murderess, came to pick winkles.

Poppies growing in a field of wheat at Adgestone. Lazy days of summer before the swallows leave and the fields are harvested.

I decide to have a look at what's left of the old church of St. Helen's at Node's Point, a white-painted sea-mark in transit with another aid to navigation, the triangular Ashey Down seamark. It appears it was purely by chance that a sailor discovered the stones from the ruined church could be used for scouring a ship's wooden decks, still called 'holy stoning' in the Navy today.

The Island, of course, has always had strong connections with the Royal Navy and words like 'nipper', used a lot in Island parlance and meaning a boy or lad, comes from the days when a boy on board a ship 'nipped' the anchor chain as it was hauled up. Another word is 'caulkhead', used to describe an Islander. There are many theories about the origin of this word, one that it comes from 'caulking' the deck of a ship, another that it's 'corkhead' with the derogatory story that all the corkheads will float when the Island sinks from an overload of tourists.

I leave the car in the National Trust car park on the Duver, or dover from the old French word 'douvre', and a name used in the south of England meaning a narrow sandy spit. C.J. Cornish, in the book he published in 1878 about the reclamation of Brading Harbour, talks of rare plants growing on the sea-sand which has gradually drifted over the Duver. The largest area of sand dunes on the Isle of Wight, it's been designated a Site of Special Scientific Interest and with 250 different species of plants, is a botanist's paradise. And here's something that gladdens my heart - the Duver was donated by the Royal Isle of Wight Golf Club "to be kept as an open space for all time." The golf course has disappeared but the place is still special for its wild flowers in the Spring and I find patches of *Armeria maritima,* or sea thrift, growing among the close cropped turf and on the beach, the silver-grey sea holly, *Eryngium maritimum.* Marbled white butterflies (an early name for this species was "Our Half Mourner" because of its chequered colouring) flit among the grasses and swallows, wheatears and redstarts are regular summer visitors to the site.

The old Southern Railway carriages have been converted into beach huts and once a year at very low spring tide, you can walk across the causeway from Bembridge to St. Helen's fort which guards the entrance to Bembridge harbour, another of Palmerston's Follies. Hundreds of people join in the annual walk to the fort and back, marching into the sea fully clothed, to the amazement of bystanders who don't know what's happening. It's getting late and a chill breeze ripples across the water. I shiver and remember the tale about the little ferry which used to run between the Duver and Bembridge Point and the ghostly passenger in black who always disappeared when the boat was in mid-stream. I look nervously over my shoulder and hurry back to the car.

But I can't leave St. Helen's without finding out more about the Dawes family. Dicky Dawes was a notorious smuggler who revelled in outsailing the Excise men by nipping through a dangerous channel between the rocks marked on Admiralty charts today as 'Dicky Dawes Gut', rather than sink a line of tubs called a crop in Priory Bay. Sophie, his daughter, helped the family's income by winkle picking in Priory Bay, a wooded Bay near Old St. Helen's church. But after Dicky Dawes died from drinking too much of the brandy he'd brought from France, the family were sent to the House of Industry, a workhouse at Parkhurst. Sophie, however, had other ideas and took off for London where her good looks were spotted by the Duc de Bourbon who educated her and made her his mistress.

When the Duc returned to France Sophie followed and, for the sake of propriety, was installed in his Paris household as his illegitimate daughter married to an officer in the King Louis XVIII's Guards. Alas, this wasn't enough for the scheming Sophie who had her eye on the Prince's money (the Duc had inherited the title and a fortune when his father died) and before he could alter his will leaving her a nice big legacy, the unfortunate man died in suspicious circumstances.

Already divorced by her husband who had discovered the truth about Sophie's relationship with the Prince and her other lovers, she was sent to trial for the Prince's murder. Things looked black for Sophie until the king intervened and she was saved from the guillotine but shunned by French society. She returned to London where she died in 1840. I think Sophie would be tickled pink if she could see the blue plaque above the door of a cottage at Upper Green in St. Helens in memory of Dicky Dawes daughter, a local girl who made bad and ended up as 'Madame de Fouchères, Queen of Chantilly'.

This a place to search for shells, to explore rock pools or to relax and listen to the waves breaking on the shore.
Priory Bay

CHAPTER FIVE

Lords and Ladies

People make history. On my journey round the Island I've learned about poets and pirates, soldiers and smugglers, a curate who liked fossils and a local girl who became a courtesan at the French court. But what about the people who governed the Island - the Lords of the Island, its Captains and governors?

To find the answer, I head for Havenstreet and the Island's county town, Newport. The deer in Combley Great Wood are hiding in its green depths, like the wallaby who, many years ago, escaped from a local wildlife park and was seen hopping along the road by a man driving home after a good evening at the pub. Rumour has it that he took the Pledge and the story may be true because a marsupial's skeleton was later found in the wood.

The Isle of Wight Council's flag flies over County Hall as I drive into Coppins Bridge roundabout. "All this beauty is of God" is the motto on the Island's coat-of-arms and the Council has a framed resolution acknowledging the relationship with our American cousins, the Isle of Wight County, Virginia, who gave us, as a permanent reminder of the "very strong friendship links between the two counties," an eighty-year-old peanut planter.

Newport owes its origins to the River Medina which rises near St. Catherine's Down and flows through Newport to Cowes and the Solent. Little is known about the river before the Normans came to the Island but there was probably a ford, or Pyle, beyond its navigable head. After Carisbrooke Castle was built, ships began to moor in the sheltered point where the Lukely Brook joins the river and around

Built in the 1100s, Carisbrooke Castle is one of the most impressive Norman castles in Britain. The gatehouse which originally had three portcullis, is fronted by two drum towers – a popular nesting place for the jackdaws.

Designed and built by John Nash, the stately Guildhall
in Newport stands on the site of the old Town Hall
and today houses the Museum of Island History.

The Tudor gateway to Church Litten where the plague victims were buried.
Inside is a simple monument to Valentine Gray, a local climbing boy who
died from being beaten by his employer, a chimney sweep.
Newport.

1180 Richard de Redvers, Lord of the Isle of Wight, founded the 'new port'. The town's streets were planned in a grid pattern based on the two original roads with three squares for market places.

The Shambles, the butchers' market and the fish market were on the north side of St. Thomas's Square. In medieval times the roads would have smelt of meat being roasted, beer being brewed, rotting vegetables and horse-dung; roads that were decked on May Day with branches from Parkhurst Forest "to refresh ye streets and ... to give a commodius and pleasant umbrage to their howses". Where wooden carts trundled across the cobbles and carriages and hansom cabs carried their passengers, Newport's streets today are busy with buses and cars.

The stately Guildhall in the High Street with its portico and Ionic colonnade was designed and built by John Nash and stands on the site of the old Town Hall and Cheese Cross. It houses the Museum of Island History where I spend an hour studying watercolour sketches made by Thomas Rowlandson, Samuel Howitt and other contemporary artists in the 1790s. What fascinates me is the detail, especially when I find a sketch of soldiers chatting to ladies in Newport with the old town hall and an arcaded market in the background.

After a peek into Island life in the 18th century, I wander into St. Thomas's Square to look at a house with "God's Providence is my Inheritance" engraved on a tablet over the door: it was at a house formerly on this site, that an outbreak of the plague is supposed to have stopped in 1584. The culprit was the black rat, 'rattus rattus', a host for the fleas that carry the plague bacillus and as the best method of moving people and goods in those days was by sea or river, it seems likely that the infected rats were brought to the Island by ship.

Across South Street, I see the Tudor gateway leading to Church Litten Park where the plague victims were buried as the parish church of St. Thomas à Becket had no burial ground. This hiccup was due to our old friend Richard de Redvers who around 1180 granted the town its first charter but when it came to building a church, somehow omitted to provide an endowment. For many years St. Thomas's remained a chapelry of the parish of Carisbrooke, first of the Priory of St. Mary and then of the church of St. Mary the Virgin, which held the right of burial for the people of Newport.

But when the plague reached Newport, the villagers of Carisbrooke made it abundantly clear they didn't want the victims buried in their graveyard and that is how Church Litten, a field outside Newport used for archery practice, came to be a burial ground. Sir Edward Horsey, a Governor of the Isle of Wight who died of the plague in 1582, has a memorial in St. Thomas's church, worth a mention because of the epitaph on his memorial. It reads, "And as he lived holily so he executed holily his particular duties."

That's not true because Sir Edward ran a sort of unofficial profitable sideline, turning a blind eye to the privateers holed up in St. Helen's and Cowes and allowing rogues and ruffians sanctuary in the part of Newport known as Castlehold. This made him popular with the Islanders who were fed-up with the French burning and pillaging their towns and villages - apparently the inhabitants of Newport didn't come near the charred remains of the town for two years after it was raided in 1377. Sir Edward also enjoyed life to the full with a young wealthy widow called Douzabelle Mill at Haseley Manor in the Arreton valley where his guests were treated to splendid meals, 'spiced up' by contributions from Horsey's fellow privateers.

St. Thomas's church survived the French raid in 1377 and moving with the times, discreetly changed its name to St. Thomas the Apostle, dropping the 'Becket' part of its name when Henry VIII announced the martyr was a traitor. In the mid-19th century the church was pulled down and in 1854 Prince Albert laid the foundation stone for a new church, later independent from Carisbrooke.

Church Litten Park is an oasis of green in the centre of Newport with trees throwing shade on the grass and the old gravestones propped against a wall. I stop in front of the simple monument to Valentine Gray, a local climbing boy who cleaned chimneys in Newport and died in 1822 as a

One famous resident at Carisbrooke Castle was
Charles I, imprisoned here in 1648. The bowling green,
which was constructed for his recreation, is used
nowadays as a venue for a Grand Medieval Joust and
other events.

Seventy-one steps lead up to the top of the keep which William FitzOsbern
built on a huge chalk mound. The castle was besieged in 1136 and forced to
surrender when the well in the keep ran dry.

result of his employer's cruelty. Charles Kingsley's *'The Water Babies'*, published in 1863, roused a lot of public sympathy for climbing boys and though Kingsley had stayed with Alfred Lord Tennyson at Farringford and may have heard Valentine's story, he's more likely to have based his book on a boy who cleaned the chimneys at his home in Eversley.

The building on the corner of St. James' Street and Lugley Street is the old King James Grammer School, completed in 1618 and the place where the Treaty of Newport is supposed to have taken place in 1648. One thing's certain – the local hostelries did well with King Charles 1's Cavaliers whooping it up in the George Inn while the Parliamentary Commissioners patronised the Bugle. As for the educational side of the school, the rules stated, "That the Master, Usher and Schollers, shalbe att Schoole att Six of the Clocke in the Morning ..." No slacking there.

I set off to look for another school. Above the door of Number 62 Crocker Street, I find a clue to my search - a statue of a girl wearing a blue dress, white apron and white bonnet, the uniform of the Newport Blue School Foundation. Founded in 1764, it was a charity school for local girls to be educated and trained for domestic service. The 'blue Jenny', as she's affectionately known, has a penny in one hand for her church collection and a Bible in the other but the statue is a reproduction – the original is housed in Carisbrooke Castle Museum.

I walk through the town to Nodehill where a French raiding party was ambushed and the dead Frenchmen, the "Noddys", were buried in a mound, later known as Noddy's Hill, all of which leads me to Carisbrooke and the castle, a mile west of Newport. The bells are ringing from the church tower as I pass a sign at the bottom of the High Street announcing, "Ducks in the road!" The yard at the Eight Bells public house, once alive with the sounds of jingling horse bells and a redcoated coachman trumpeting 'Tally Ho', is full of cars. Village myth mingles with history - it's traditional for a bride to climb the worn flight of 'Wedding Steps' to the church and there's a mysterious handprint in the wall of the churchyard where a sturdy yew tree dates from the 16th century.

Evening on the River Medina. The nearby Folly Inn was built on a barge after it was damaged during a storm in the 18th century and the ship's keel timbers have been left under the pub's floor.

Buried nearby is Horatio Dennett, the man who invented the line-carrying rocket used by coastguards to rescue people marooned on wrecked vessels. The cottages by the lych gate to the church were originally the 'Cutters Arms' and it's been suggested the pub might have started life when the monks at the Priory, weary of providing free 'B and B', started charging travellers for their hospitality.

The village lies below the hill where William FitzOsbern, a crony of William the Conqueror, built the first part of his castle, the keep, in one corner of an existing Saxon burh. An anonymous historian wrote in *Gesta Stephani* that Carisbrooke Castle was "very finely built of stone and strongly fortified", a succinct description of FitzOsbern's motte-and-bailey castle.

Now, with its grey stone curtain walls weathered over the centuries, the castle is more benign than forbidding and though the grave of a Saxon woman, buried with a purse and comb, was excavated in the Privy Garden, no ghosts, Saxon or Norman, haunt the castle. It did, however, provide the right atmosphere for Shakespeare's 'Hamlet' which I saw performed in the courtyard with the ghost of Hamlet's father walking the walls and mourning, "My hour is almost come."

Carisbrooke Castle's history is linked with people like Countess Isabella de Fortibus, the last of the Island's independent rulers and known as the 'Queen of Wight', who sold the Lordship of Wight when she was dying to Edward I for the sum of 6,000 marks. And another famous but unwilling resident was the king who lost his head, Charles I, who was imprisoned here in 1648. The castle has been besieged twice, once in 1136 by King Stephen when the well in the keep ran dry and its owner, Baldwin de Redvers was forced to surrender, then again in 1377 when a French force advanced on Carisbrooke after they'd destroyed Yarmouth and Newtown.

Legend has it that a bowman called Peter de Heynoe noticed the French commander *"nyghtes and mornings neare ye Castle"* and with permission from the Captain of the Island, Sir Hugh Tyrell, killed the French leader with his crossbow (for some time described as a 'silver bow') from a loop hole on the west

The Norman's used the wood from the forests to build wooden pallisades to protect the castle.

Deer hide in the green depths of Combley Great Wood where, it's rumoured, a wallaby also took refuge after escaping from a local wildlife park.

wall of the castle. Naturally, the French soldiers were rather peeved about their commander's death so the Islanders dug deep into their pockets and paid them one thousand marks to go home.

If you don't suffer from vertigo, you can totter round the castle's walls and see what is, allegedly, 'Heynoe's loop' and on a lower level, Isabella's window in her great chamber. Isabella made a lot of improvements to her draughty home and I like to imagine her sitting at the window, looking over Carisbrooke to Parkhurst Forest and wondering when the builders would put glass in the window or which of the wines from Bordeaux to choose for dinner in the Great Hall – didn't I say people make history?

But the donkeys at Carisbrooke Castle are equally famous. After the well in the keep failed during the siege of 1136, a new well was sunk in the courtyard. Later a wellhouse was built and it may be that prisoners were used on the treadwheel which, today, is worked by donkeys. I join the queue of tourists to watch a donkey step daintily on to the treadwheel, the custodian tips a cup of water down the well and we count up to five (the time it takes the water to fall 161ft. down the well) before hearing it land at the bottom with a gentle plop. Memorials in the donkeys' little museum show that Jack and Jenny were popular names for the animals who now work to rule, each doing a ten minute stint in the wheel.

Yachts moored on the Medina. Gone are the days when the river was the only important means of communication to the Island. Today goods are carried by ferry and the river slumbers between meadows as it wends its way to the sea.

While most of the castle is under the guardianship of English Heritage, the museum in the Great Hall is administered by an independent trust founded by Princess Beatrice, the youngest daughter of Queen Victoria, in memory of her husband, Prince Henry of Battenberg. The old building provides an ideal setting for objects found or excavated at the castle, such as a 13th century wine-jug and fragments of chain mail and in a room upstairs, the cryptic letters King Charles wrote while he was held prisoner and hid for Mary, the laundress he code-named "B", to smuggle out to his friends. At that time, the castle seethed with intrigue, with Charles and his page, Henry Firebrace, plotting the king's escape and Cromwell's Parliamentary agents spying on the King's household. Firebrace had told the king that he thought the window in the king's bedroom was too narrow for Charles to squeeze through but refrained from saying, "I told you so," when the king got stuck. Alas, the window has gone – remodelled in 1856 – and I think how frustrated Firebrace must have felt while he waited in the courtyard and heard Charles groaning.

I continue to the little room where Charles's daughter, Elizabeth, died in 1650 aged fourteen after she caught a chill. Elizabeth and her brother, Prince Henry, were brought to the castle after their father was executed and a painting in the room entitled, 'The Royal Prisoners', by C.W. Pope, a

Victorian artist, catches my eye. Painted 200 years after Elizabeth's death, the artist has captured the afternoon sun slanting into the room as Prince Henry and his guard discover the dead princess with a miniature of her father in her hand. The painting is full of the symbolism beloved by the Victorians - like the open bird cage representing her spirit freed like a bird from imprisonment and the guard's broken pipe on the floor - but for all that, there's a poignancy about the picture which makes you linger over the princess's sad story. Her grave was discovered in St. Thomas's church in Newport in 1793 and when the church was rebuilt, Queen Victoria commissioned a sculpture in her memory - the musuem has a small replica on show.

A heady whiff of history lingers everywhere in the castle. I cross the courtyard to the gatehouse which Queen Elizabeth 11 drove through in 1965 to install Lord Louis Mountbatten as Governor of the Isle of Wight. A pigeon coos contentedly on its nest, perched where once Baldwin's men dropped missiles through the floor on their enemies.

I stand in the entrance to the castle looking at the pastoral view across the valley which inspired the poet John Keats to write, "A thing of beauty is a joy for ever ...". It hasn't changed so much since Isabella's day or since Sir George Carey, Elizabeth 1's cousin and governor of the Island, up-dated the castle's defences against the threat of a Spanish Armada. The past is now part of the present.

On my journey, I've discovered the Isle of Wight has its own highly distinct personality, it's a separate thing with its own traditions and appearances. It has a huge variety of scenery, history and lifestyles in a small area. The past blends with the present and the influence of the sea is never far away. It is a rare place - truly a **gem of the Solent**.

A scene with the charm of old England. The thatched cottages in Winkle Street used to be known as Barrington Row. A stream flows under a bridge to an ancient sheepwash.

Photo Notes

Before moving to the Isle of Wight in the Autumn of 2000, my ideas of what the place was like was based on a mixture of memories of my childhood and a feeling that all I would find would be kiss-me-quick hats and bottles of coloured sands. Thankfully I was quite wrong!

The island has some of the most breathtaking and photogenic scenery of the British Isles. It never ceases to amaze me how varied and diverse the photographic opportunities are on an island measuring no more than 23 miles by 13 miles. From tiny coves and sandy beaches to rolling hills and dense woodland, the Isle of Wight has it all.

After nearly 15 years of working with film, I decided last year to take the plunge into digital photography. The vast majority of pros have now made the switch, seeing the benefits of speed, convenience and above all image quality that now beats film hands down, format for format. Of course the biggest prejudice most photographers who make the switch have to contend with is "is it real photography?". To me it makes no difference if silver halides or silicon chips are used to capture the images; there is no substitute for the human eye.

I currently use a Canon EOS 1DS digital 35mm SLR, after changing from a Nikon F90X film SLR in 2002. The Canon uses a digital sensor of the same dimensions as 35mm film, allowing you to use normal 35mm lenses but giving you quality to rival medium format. A tripod is used for at least 90% of my photography, slowing down the creative process and allowing oneself the time to properly assess a scene. 'Phase Ones' excellent, 'Capture One', processing software is used for developing the images along with 'Photoshop CS' for printing. I use exactly the same techniques that I honed over 10 years in the darkroom, namely cropping, dodging and burning, and colour correction.

Steve Gascoigne
November 2004

Time and tide waits for no man and the Island's
coastline is under constant threat from the sea.
Freshwater Bay.

Isle of Wight

The end of a long day on the beach.
Appley Tower catches the last of the evening
sunset as night creeps in from the sea.

Bibliography & Links

Du Boulay, Ernest	**Bembridge Past and Present** (1911)
Cornish, C.J.	**The Reclamation of Brading Harbour** (Strand Press, 1878)
Hyland, Paul	**Wight: Biography of an Island** (Victor Gollancz Ltd., 1984) *A comprehensive and interesting guide to the Isle of Wight*
Jones, Jack	**Isle of Wight Curiosities** (The Dovecote Press, 1989) *A delightful collection of extraordinary stories about the Island*
Jones, Jack	**The Royal Prisoner** (Lutterworth Press, 1965) *Written by a former curator of Carisbrooke Castle Museum, Dr. J.D. Jones'* *book is a documented account of Charles I's imprisonment*
Medland, J.C.	**Shipwrecks of the Wight** (Coach House Publications Ltd., 2004) *An insight into the Island's treacherous coastal waters.*
Winter, C.W.R.	**Colourful Characters of the Isle of Wight** (Coach House Publications Ltd., 1997) *Some of the men and women who have played a part in the* *Island's history*

Links

To contact the photographer or obtain prints of the photographs in this book,
please feel free to visit: **www.AvailableLightPhotography.co.uk**

Further copies of the book are available online from: **www.coachhouseonline.co.uk**

Isle of Wight Tourist Board: **www.islandbreaks.co.uk**
For practical information on visiting the Island.

Isle of Wight Coastal Visitors Centre: **www.coastalwight.gov.uk**

Carisbrooke Castle Museum: **www.carisbrookecastlemuseum.org.uk**

Bembridge lifeboat, the 24-ton *Max Aitken 111*, was donated to the RNLI in 1987 by the Beaverbrook Foundation in memory of Lord Beaverbrook.
Before the lifeboat station was built, the lifeboat was launched from the beach and on its return, pulled back by six horses.